PAPADAKIS/MELETZIS

EPIDAUROS

P9-BJU-135

EPIDAUROS

THE SANCTUARY OF ASCLEPIOS

TEXT
THEODORE PAPADAKIS

PHOTOGRAPHS
SPYROS MELETZIS
HELEN PAPADAKIS

VERLAG SCHNELL & STEINER MÜNCHEN · ZÜRICH
ART EDITIONS MELETZIS & PAPADAKIS · ATHENS

All photographs by Spyros Meletzis and Helen Papadakis, Athens. The designs of the sanctuary by Aristoteles Papadakis, Athens, according to P. Cavvadias, the map of p. 24 by the layouter. The front cover shows the Theatre and its monumental western entrance, the back cover a modern performance of a tragedy by Aeschylos in the ancient Theatre.

6th EDITION 1978, COMPLETELY NEW COMPOSED   ISBN 3 7954 0804 0

SOLE DISTRIBUTOR FOR GREECE: HELEN PAPADAKIS, 15 PEFKON ST., ATHENS 625

© 1978 BY SCHNELL & STEINER MUNICH & ZURICH AND ART EDITIONS MELETZIS & PAPADAKIS ATHENS. — ALL RIGHTS RESERVED. — LAYOUT BY DR. JOHANNES STEINER MUNICH. — PRINTED IN ITALY BY KINA ITALIA S.P.A., MILANO, IN COLLABORATION WITH SCHNELL & STEINER WALDSASSEN, GERMANY

Sanctuary of Asklepios — Reconstruction of the main buildings (A. Defrasse)

EPIDAUROS

THE SANCTUARY OF ASCLEPIOS

At the entrance of the sacred grove of the ancient sanctuary of Asclepios at Epidauros, upon the architrave of the majestic Propylaea, forming almost an arch of triumph, with two rows of marble columns, 6 Ionian on the outer side and 6 Corinthian on the inner side, the following rythmed words were inscribed:

»ΑΓΝΟΝ ΧΡΗ ΝΗΟΙΟΣ ΘΗΩΔΕΟΣ ΕΝΤΟΣ ΙΟΝΤΑ ΕΜΜΕΝΑΙ ΑΓΝΕΙΗ Δ ΕΣΤΙ ΦΡΟΝΕΙΝ ΟΣΙΑ«

which means:

" Pure must be he who enters the fragrant temple;
Purity means to think nothing but holy thoughts ".

This inscription, though not preserved but known to us from many ancient writers and travellers, reveals the true character and the primary destination of the most famous of the Asclepieia of the ancient world and presents in their true light the wonderful healings effected there; these cures which restored not only the physical health but also the psychic harmony of the pilgrim, regenerating him completely.

The Asclepieion of Epidauros, this religious institution of higher spirituality and artistic beauty, with its remarkable achievements for the physical and spiritual reformation of men, has not ceased to attract the interest of many thinkers and scientists and justifies its world renown and its long and glorious history (from the end of the 6th century B. C. to the end of the 5th A. D.).

This "φρονεῖν ὅσια" reminds us of the words of Jesus Christ "φρονεῖς τά τοῦ Θεοῦ" (" Think as God thinks ", Mark 8:33), and of St Paul "τά ἄνω φρονεῖτε" (" Let your thoughts dwell on that higher realm ", Col 3:2) and "τό φρόνημα τοῦ πνεύματος ζωή καί εἰρήνη" (" Have the spiritual outlook that is life and peace ", Rom 8:6, NEB, Oxford and Cambridge UP).

From the first moment, one feels that one is entering a sacred and spiritual place. One must forget all material preoccupations and lift oneself spiritually, holding in one's mind only holy and beautiful thoughts. Here reigns life immortal and perfectly harmonious; neither death nor birth is seen. Only Life, without beginning or end.

The god who is worshipped here is Asclepios, the god of health, the " Soter " (" Saviour "), the " Philanthropotatos " (" the most manloving ") of all the gods of the ancient Greeks. He is good and " Epikouros " (" assistant ") and has so much affection for men that he helps them in all circumstances, healing them from any kind of disease, and he would certainly have liberated them even from death, if Zeus had not intervened personally to restore the unsearchable divine order.

The worship of Asclepios became quickly pan-Hellenic and spread all over the Roman empire. Asclepios survived more than anyother of the Olympian or other gods of the ancient world, even some centuries after the predominance of Christianity. Maximos, the biographer of the neoplatonic philosopher Proclos, writing after 485 A. D., relates that at this date " the sanctuary of the Saviour " remained " unconquered ".

The Greeks, especially after the disastrous Peloponnesian War (431—404 B. C.) were in great need of gods like Dionysos and Asclepios, whom they felt were much closer to them than the magnificent Olympian gods. So they turned more and more to Asclepios, who became the god " EVERGETES " (" benefactor "), " EPIKOOS " (" understanding "), " PHILOLAOS " (" friend of the people "), " EFKOLOS " (" easy "), as they called him; the practical god, supporting men in their daily life and always available for all their needs.

Asclepios became, substituting gradually even Apollo, the god of health and medicine. But not only of medicine as we understand it nowadays, which cures the body with remedies and other material means, but mainly the god of " NOOTHÉRAPIA " (" Mind-Healing "), who purifies and reforms the entire human being, both body and mind, using exclusively mental means and the spiritual power of the divine, like Jesus Christ.

Asclepios is thus recognized as the god protector not only of medical science, which, starting from his own sons, Machaon and Podalairios and the long row of famous " Asclepiades " (physicians), among whom Hippocrates, the father of medicine, comes down to our times, but also of the Asclepieia, where his priests effected " miraculous " cures, with the sole use of the " admirable divine power ", as it is officially stressed in the first of the two stelae of healing which were found in Epidauros and are now exhibited in the local Museum.

These stelae were found during the excavations which the Greek Archaeological Society has executed at Epidauros, since 1881 under the eminent archaeologist P. Cavvadias, who made it his life-long task (he died in 1928) to bring to life the entire sanctuary of Asclepios, which today is one of the places most worth seeing in Greece, for its magnificent monuments and art treasures.

The excavations were continued even after the death of Cavvadias by John Papadimitriou and other distinguished Greek archaeologists, who searched more thoroughly the very ancient temple of Apollo Maleatas on Mount Kynortion and proved its close connection with the Hieron of Asclepios. (The pilgrims of Asclepios had to offer a preliminary sacrifice to Apollo Maleatas at his temple, the offerings were shared between the two shrines and the cures were officially attributed to the dual healing power of both these gods or rather to their triune power, since hero Maleatas who had merged with Apollo was also known especially for his outstanding therapeutic capacities).

The greatest success, however, of the excavations was the discovery of the two marble stelae already mentioned, where are inscribed in detail 43 cases of healings which occurred at the Asclepieion of Epidauros before the 2nd half of the 4th c. B. C. These cures are remarkable and raise a great scientific problem, because they surpass by far the achievements of the medical science of today. They concern diseases for us incurable (even of people blind from birth, the lame and paralytic) which are healed instantly, without remedies or ohter material means, even from a distance, with the sole use of the " admirable divine power ". There were many such tablets of healings in the sanctuary, as we know from Pausanias, who visited Epidauros about the year 150 A. D., though at his time only six of them were left.

The study of these tablets reveals to us (and this revelation is important if it leads us to investigate this problem more scientifically), that during the first, and the most glorious, period of the history of the Asclepieion of Epidauros (i. e. up to the end, at least, of the 4th century B. C., when the stelae were inscribed) the healings were not obtained by medicines or other material means, but by the sole supernatural healing power of the divine Mind — that power, which the priests of Asclepios knew from times of old, adored respectfully, preserved by secret tradition and utilized for therapeutic purposes.

Judging from the results they reached, (for which there should not be the slightest doubt, as they were recorded in the most responsible way on the tablets preserved), we must admit that the priests of Asclepios, who were not physicians but profound thinkers, had advanced more than contemporary science in matters of " NOOTHERAPY " (" Mind-healing "), of psychosomatic and generally in the search and the comprehension of the spiritual laws regulating the universe. Surely they knew more than we do about the great influence exerted by the divine Harmony and Order on the psychic harmony and the physical health of men, and about the unlimited possibilities of spiritualized thought for the restoration of the body and the mind. And the most important is that the priests of Asclepios had discovered and perfected the practical methods for the application of their knowledge in order to effect their " miraculous " cures. They considered it fundamental to teach men to think only holy thoughts (" FRONEIN OSIA ") because they believed, and they proved it, that when our thought is maintained in a pure and harmonious state, then necessarily even our body becomes healthy and harmonious.

The divine Plato, who had a very high esteem for the medical science or " art ", and believed that the state of health is the only really natural condition of man, which could only temporarily be disturbed by morbid disharmonies, relates the following most enlightening views on Asclepios' method, in his dialogue Symposium (186 d, e). Speaking through the mouth of the physician-philosopher Eryximachos, the descendant of an old and distinguished family of doctors, he says: " Medicine must, indeed, be able to make the most hostile elements in the body friendly and loving towards each other ... It was by knowing the means by which to introduce " Eros " and harmony in these that, as the poets here say and I also believe, our forefather Asclepios established this science (art) of ours ". (tr. Sykoutris and Lamb). And he continues by mentioning music, gymnastics, harmony, agriculture, etc. as the " means ".

In conformity thus with the great tradition of Asclepios, his priests, (who were the first to maintain themselves on a very high level of spirituality), used every means conducive to the strengthening of the natural impulse (or " Eros " according to Plato) of the human soul towards the beautiful, the good and the divine, in order to put the pilgrim's thought in line with the spiritual reality. They were thus " awakening " him to his real self (" GNOTHI SAFTON " or " KNOW THYSELF ") and regenerating him both physically and spiritually.

Primarily, of course, they exalted and fortified, with the appropriate ceremonies, worship, hymns and " doxologies ", the religious sentiments of the pilgrims and their deep faith and trust in the Divine Order, the great gods and especially towards Asclepios, the absolutely good and the most philanthropist of all gods, the " Saviour ", who had the power to free them from every evil, suffering or sickness.

They used, besides, the harmony and rhythm in music, dance and poetry, for their character building efficacy and for the immediate healing influence they exerted upon the mind and body. But also ancient tragedy and comedy, and epic and lyric poetry, because they increased the spirituality and the purification of the soul from the destructive passions. Gymnastics and athletic games were also utilized, because they disciplined the movements and the inner rhythm of the body, strengthening, at the same time, the psychic and the physical capacities of man. And, lastly, the artistic creation, the contemplation and enjoyment of the beautiful, through the masterpieces of architecture, sculpture and painting, because they were considered an important factor for the elevation and spiritualization of human thought and the restoration of the health of both mind and body. They actually believed that the active contemplation of the beautiful and the good brings harmony and health to every individual. The more man's thought communes with the divine harmony, the more spiritual, powerful and healthy he becomes.

And thus, ascending, step by step, the scale of Diotima, we can reach to the contemplation of the absolutely beautiful and good.

It is not possible to deal here more in extension with these ideas, which, from Pythagoras to Plato and Plotinus, nurtured the ancient Greeks; (they can be found in the dialogues of Plato, e. g. Ion, the Symposium, Phaedros, the Republic, the Laws, etc.). Still, extremely interesting is the investigation of the way in which these ideas were put into application in the Asclepieion of Epidauros and of the wonderful results obtained there.

The few explanations given above were thought necessary to solve the perplexity of the modern visitor who may not understand why in this Asclepieion (erroneously described by some as a therapeutic institution, a sanatorium or a Spa, or even a combination of the above with the shrines of the Holy Virgin of Tinos or of Lourdes) were gathered so many wonderful monuments and masterpieces of Greek art. The most beautiful theatre of ancient Greece, work of the famous sculptor and architect Polycleitos the Younger; the gracious Tholos, renowned for its excellent architecture and its magnificent sculptured and painted decorations; statues by famous artists like Thrasymedes and Theodotos, and beside the majestic temple of Asclepios and of Artemis, a large Gymnasium, an Odeion, a Library, a Stadium, etc.

All these are the "means" mentioned by Plato, the medical instruments we might say today, to "introduce" Eros and harmony into the soul of the pilgrim and so make him more spiritual and receptive to the healing influence of the divine Mind. The history of the Asclepieion of Epidauros lasted, as we have seen, for almost a millenium. During the first heroic centuries of its greatest glory, the healing means used were exclusively spiritual; later on, however, when the spirituality and the faith in the omnipotence of the divine weakened, they started to use even here, auxiliarily, some remedies (supposedly prescribed by the god himself), which, during Roman times, were generalized, comprising the most modern means of hygiene, dietetics, surgical operations, bath therapies, purgatives, etc. At the Asclepieia of these times, apart from the priesthood, were to be found real physicians, who took advantage of the great crowds of sick people flocking there to practise and perfect their science. Nevertheless, the Hieron of Epidauros maintained a great reputation up to its last days, and wonderful cures were effected there.

The worshippers of Asclepios were not uneducated, naïve or credulous people; they were even very distinguished men of great culture, like the tragic poet Aristarchos, the writer of comedies Theopombos, the orator Aristides, the philosopher Crantor, the senator Antonius, etc. Names even more famous are mentioned, that of the philosopher and emperor Marcus Aurelius and of the great tragedian Sophocles, who, besides, ministered personally as a priest at the Asclepieion of Athens and composed a well-known paean in honour of the god, which was sung for many centuries in the Asclepieia, but has unfortunately not been preserved.

The mere name of the great Sophocles is sufficient to show of what higher standing and spirituality were the priests of the Asclepieia. And let us remember that to Asclepios of all gods was addressed the last thought, a few moments before his death, of the greatest of the philosophers, Socrates. And it was a thought of gratitude: " Crito ", he said, " we owe a cock to Asclepios. Pay it and do not neglect it " (Phaedo, 118 a).

ASCLEPIOS (AESCULAPIUS) IN MYTHOLOGY

Many legends and myths were created in ancient times about the birth and origin of the good Hero-God Asclepios, the Saviour and protector of the oppressed, the great Healer of bodies and souls. Many regions and cities of Greece claimed the glory of being his birthplace. More prominent were the Thessalian Trikki, Epidauros, Messina and Arcadia.

According to the oldest tradition, the native land of Asclepios was Trikki (today Trikkala) of Thessaly, where was located the oldest Sanctuary for his worship. In later times, however, the Hieron of Epidauros in Argolid became the most important and famous centre in the whole of Greece for the cult of Asclepios, as Delphi was for Apollo, and so naturally the local tradition of Epidauros prevailed that the god was born on Mount Titthion, not far from this sanctuary. (The Asclepieion of Epidauros was the metropolis from which originated the most important of the more than 300 Asclepieia of the ancient world, like that of Athens (since 420 B. C.), Sicyon, Cos, Pergamum (3rd cent. B. C.), Knidos, Rome (since 293 B. C.), Taranta, Cyrene, etc.).

The ancient, great poets, Homer, Hesiod and Pindar mention Asclepios as an excellent hero physician ("ἀμύνων ἰητήρ"), whose two sons, Machaon and Podalairios, took part in the war of Troy as Thessalian kings and distinguished themselves for their valor and the medical art they had from their father.

Asclepios probably lived during the 13th century B. C.; he is mentioned among the heros of the Argonautic expedition, together with Jason, Heracles, the Dioscuroi and others. There is even a tradition that 53 years before the Trojan war, he climbed up Mount Olympus, together with Heracles.

According to the Thessalian legend, sung by Pindar in

his beautiful 3rd Pythian, Asclepios was the son of Apollo and Coronis, the most beautiful daughter of the king of Thessaly, Phlegyas. The pretty virgin was bathing one day in the Boebian lake when Apollo saw her and immediately fell in love and united with her. But as Pindar says, " whereas she already had in her womb the fruit of the love of the bright god ", she disdained the love of the god for a mortal, a stranger from Arcadia, Ischys, the son of Elatos.

Apollo learned about the betrayal of his beloved from the crow, or, as Pindar believes, he guessed it by himself. He became so angry that he immediately turned the unfortunate bird from white to black, killed his rival Ischys and asked his sister Artemis to shoot the unfaithful Coronis with her arrows. But at the moment her parents were about to burn the body of the poor princess upon a pyre, Phoebus remembered that in her womb she had his son Asclepios. He dashed (or rather he sent Hermes, as Pausanias says) and snatched the babe out of the flames and brought it to Chiron, the famous Centaur and teacher, who lived on Pelion, the mount with the luxurious vegetation and the invigorating air. This wise Centaur, who was " full of love for men ", as Pindar says, had brought up a lot of famous heroes and demigods, like Heracles, Jason, Amphiaraos, the Dioscuroi, Peleas and his glorious son Achilleus and many others. Chiron had a great passion for nature and hunting, but he was also an excellent musician and a physician who had made extensive researches on the healing capacities of all the herbs of Pelion.

Chiron was immortal, but he magnanimously gave up his immortality for the benefit of another great benefactor of mankind, Prometheus, who had dared to set himself even against the will of the gods for what he thought was good for the human race. For this superb deed, Zeus transformed Chiron into the constellation of Sagittarius and placed him in heaven to shine there eternally.

Asclepios soon became more famous than his teacher, effecting the most remarkable healings, by his sole appearance and the great love he had for all mankind; sometimes, however, he used various herbs or medicines and made surgical operations. He accompagnied as a physician the heroes who took part in the expedition to Colchis under Jason; he healed Heracles and Iphikleus from the poisoneous bites of the Lernea Hydra, the daughters of king Proitos from mania, the king of Epidauros Ascles and others. According to the legend, he even succeeded in raising the dead, like Glafkos the son of Minos, Hippolytos the son of Theseus, the hero Lycurgos, Tyndareos, etc.

But when he exceeded measure (this first virtue of the Greeks) and continued to resuscitate a lot of people, Pluto, the god of Hades, protested to Zeus, who, fearing that the Order of the world might be shaken, struck down Asclepios with a thunderbolt. Having thus died as a martyr for the good of humanity, Asclepios was deified and became the god of health and of medicine, the " Saviour " of mankind.

According to the tradition of Epidauros related by Pausanias, Asclepios was born in the vicinity of the Hieron of Epidauros, on mount Myrtion, since named Titthion,

which means " the mountain which gave the breast ". This is a charming variation, which binds the god more closely with his most famous Asclepieion and with the localities, the men and the animals of this area, restoring, at the same time, the dignity and purity of his mother, who knew only Apollo.

The king of Thessaly, Phlegyas, wanted to conquer the whole of the Peloponnese. In order to reconnoitre the country, he took his beautiful daughter and they came as tourists to the pleasant area of Epidauros. But as soon as they arrived there, Coronis, who, without her father's knowledge, had had relations with the god Apollo, gave birth secretly to Asclepios and concealed him on the mountain overlooking the actual Hieron. The divine child was suckled by a goat and guarded by a shepherd's dog. One day, shepherd Aristhenas, looking after his two animals, found the baby and tried to touch it. But as he approached " he saw the sparkle of lightning " radiating from the child and he understood that it was a divine child. So the news spread immediately " in every land and sea ", says Pausanias, that a god had been born who could heal all kind of diseases and even raise the dead. Since then, the dog and the goat became the sacred animals of Asclepios and his sanctuary was erected between the two mountains, the Titthion which gave him the breast and the Kynortion (from the word " dog ") where was the very old shrine of Maleatas Apollo.

During the 3rd century B. C., the Epidaurian poet Isyllos improved this version of Epidauros and, with the approval of the Oracle of Delphi, which always supported Epidauros, he dedicated a marble stele to the gods Apollo and Asclepios, and placed it in the Hieron so that everybody might know the true birthplace of the god. (This stele has been preserved in very good condition and is now exhibited in the Museum of Epidauros).

According to Isyllos, it was not by chance that Asclepios was born in the area of Epidauros. His own mother originated from this locality, being the daughter of Cleophama, the daughter of the Muse Erato and Malos, the son of Zeus, who erected the sanctuary of Maleatas Apollo on mount Kynortion. Cleophama married Phlegyas, who was also from Epidauros, and they had a daughter Aigle, surnamed, for her great beauty, Coronis. With this Aigle or Coronis of Epidauros Apollo fell in love and he chose her to give birth to the beneficent god Asclepios.

The birth of the divine child took place, as Pausanias relates, within the sacred grove of the Hieron and the goddess Artemis and all the Moirai assisted at this event.

*

We can follow in these graceful traditions how a god is born and formed in order to meet the deepest and more spiritual needs of men, and how from the Olympian gods, rather cruel and full of passions, we attain the supreme good, the immaculate and beneficent, the absolutely pure and harmonious Asclepios.

As a hero who was deified, Asclepios participates of both natures, the human and the divine; he symbolizes the inseparable unity existing between them and is the way leading from the one to the other. Even in historic times, Asclepios' identity was always ambiguous between a god and a hero, and he was offered at the same time sacrifices appropriate to a god and " ENAGISMA-TA " for a hero. (This secret worship of the hero Asclepios was effected, in our opinion, in the famous Tholos of Epidauros, in its mysterious subterranean labyrinth, where, most probably, a snake symbolizing Asclepios was kept. So the Temple was for the god and the nearby Tholos for the hero).

Asclepios, however, is mainly known as the great healer. The practical and living god, who expresses the healing action of the divine. The Truth which frees and heals. In this capacity, Asclepios the " Saviour " attained great renown all over the ancient world. His cult outlived, as we have seen, any other of the ancient world, long after the Olympian gods were forgotten and even some centuries after the predominance of Christianity.

In his famous apologetic work for Christianity " Against Celsus ", which the great Alexandrine Origenes wrote in 248 A. D., we see that it is Asclepios who is chosen as the more worthy of all the ancient gods to be somehow compared with Jesus Christ. Christ and Asclepios are compared for their great healing power, for their perfectly pure life and because, contrary to the other ancient religions and " mysteries ", which invited only the pure and the good, they did not exclude from salvation the sinners, who most of all needed their help. From this dispute and from the remarks of Origenes we can see how greatly the ancient world respected Asclepios and believed in his wonderful healings (Origines " Against Celsus ", Book III, Chapters 22—25).

In ancient Greek art, Asclepios is represented as an earnest man, with a handsome beard, thick hair and a serene and majestic expression. He is wearing a large " himation ", which leaves bare his breast. His physiognomy ressembles strangely that of Zeus, especially during the later period, when his fame had spread beyond the frontiers of Greece. But his powerful and earnest figure was always illumined with goodness. (During the 4th century A. D., a statue found in Panea — the Kaisaria of Philippoi — was supposed to represent Jesus Christ, while it was of Asclepios. According to one theory, the face of Jesus, which predominated in art after the middle of the 5th century A. D., was inspired by the face of Asclepios, and this explains why it ceased to be youthful, as it was during the first centuries).

The distinctive symbols of Asclepios are his sacred animals and the staff he holds in his hand with a snake coiled around it. The most usual are the snake and the dog symbolizing the local (chthonios) god. The goat, the staff and the diadem symbolize his benevolence. His medical capacity is also sometimes represented by rolls of papyri, boxes of ointments, vials, etc.

The sacred snakes, which symbolized the god himself and his healing power (still today they are the symbol of the medical profession) were kept in great numbers in the Asclepieia. According to the legend, Asclepios had himself nurtured this animal on Mount Pelion; it symbolized the ever regenerating life. The snakes of Epidauros had a yellow-brown colour and were called " pareiai ". They were harmless and circulated freely in the sanctuary and in the temple. Sometimes, they were enormous, as Pausanias says.

For the establishment of a new Asclepieion, a snake was sent from Epidauros, which was received as the god himself. Such snakes were sent for the erection of the Asclepieia of Cos, Ephesus and Rome. The first serpent destined for Cos escaped from the ship near the coast of eastern Laconia and landed at the point where Epidauros Limira was founded.

The Romans, as related by Livius (X, 48), after a great epidemic and upon the advice of the Sibylline Books, sent a delegation to Epidauros in 293 B. C. to get a sacred serpent. But before its return to Rome, the serpent escaped and, swimming up the River Tiber, reached the sacred island across the Capitol, where the Asclepieion of Rome was built.

Asclepios was surrounded by many secondary divinities, which were related to his healing power. Epione, his wife, his daughters Hygieia, Aigle, Panacea or Iaso and his son Telesphoros, who helps convalescents and was worshipped, with Machaon, Hypnos (sleep) and Oniros (dream) in the temple of the " Epidotes " in the Hieron, as mentioned by Pausanias.

In many places, Asclepios was worshipped in common with Apollo or with Athena. In Epidauros we see the amalgamation of the healing power of three famous healers: Apollo, the local hero Maleatas and Asclepios, who finally predominated. In Athens, the cult of Asclepios had been introduced from Epidauros, since 420 B. C. The Asclepieion was near the Acropolis. His worship had been combined with the worship of the Eleusinian goddesses Demeter and Persephone and a day of the Great Eleusinians was dedicated to the god Asclepios and named Epidauria.

*

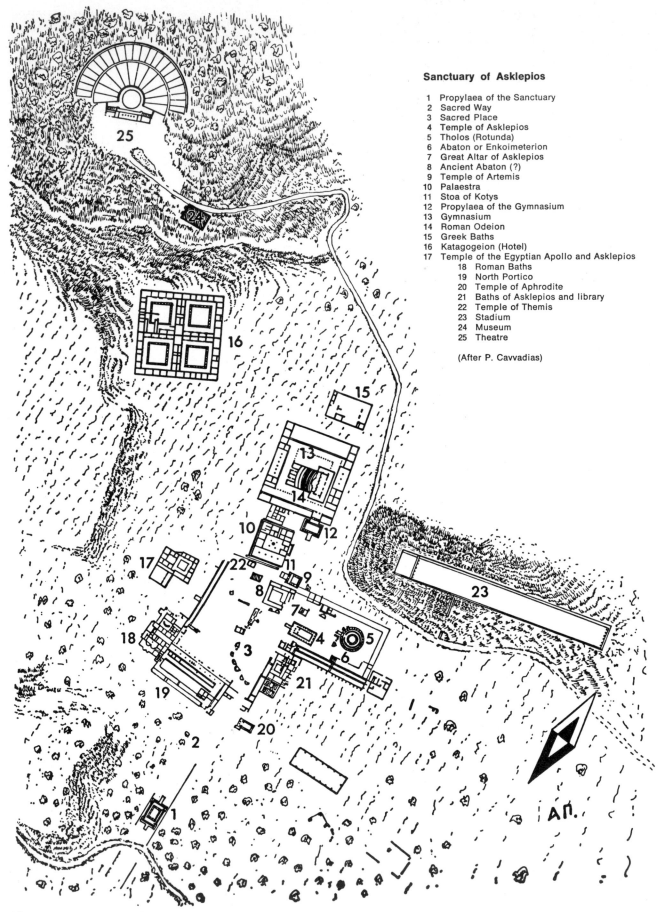

Sanctuary of Asklepios

1 Propylaea of the Sanctuary
2 Sacred Way
3 Sacred Place
4 Temple of Asklepios
5 Tholos (Rotunda)
6 Abaton or Enkoimeterion
7 Great Altar of Asklepios
8 Ancient Abaton (?)
9 Temple of Artemis
10 Palaestra
11 Stoa of Kotys
12 Propylaea of the Gymnasium
13 Gymnasium
14 Roman Odeion
15 Greek Baths
16 Katagogeion (Hotel)
17 Temple of the Egyptian Apollo and Asklepios
18 Roman Baths
19 North Portico
20 Temple of Aphrodite
21 Baths of Asklepios and library
22 Temple of Themis
23 Stadium
24 Museum
25 Theatre

(After P. Cavvadias)

DESCRIPTION OF THE SACRED PRECINCTS

The cult of Asclepios at Epidauros dates from the end of the 6th century B. C. But from prehistoric times Apollo Maleatas was worshipped in this area and his sanctuary on Mount Kynortion has been preserved.

During the 5th c. B. C., the Asclepieion had already acquired a great renown for the " miraculous " cures effected there and for its festivals and games, which attracted many visitors from all over Greece. The principal festival of the Hieron was the " Asclepieia ", later named the " Great Asclepieia ", which took place every four years, 9 days after the Isthmian Games, during the months of April to June. At the beginning, there were only " gymnic " games, but later they added contests of rhapsodies and music (related by Plato) and even dramatic competitions and chariot races.

In the 4th c. B. C., the Hieron had become so prosperous that it was decided to renovate it completely. The best artists and architects of the time were called and they constructed the wonderful monuments which have survived till now.

Up to the Hellenistic period, the Asclepieion of Epidauros remained intact and in high esteem, as related by Aemilius Paulus, who visited it in the year 167 B. C.

But in 86 B. C. the Hieron was sacked by Sulla, who plundered all the sanctuaries of Greece (as Delphi, Olympia, the Acropolis, etc.) to wage his war against king Mithridates. And these devastations were followed by repeated incursions of Cilician pirates.

Very quickly, however, the Hieron of Epidauros recovered its old fame, and was even supported by the Romans. About the middle of the 2nd c. A. D., the Roman senator Antonius erected, at his own expense, many new buildings and repaired the old ones. When Pausanias visited Epidauros in the year 150 A. D., the shrine was in full prosperity, though its initial aspect had been altered because of its invasion by many foreign gods and demons.

The description given by Pausanias will help us to reconstruct in our imagination the grandeur of the Hieron of Epidauros, before we visit it in its actual state, after approximately 1820 years, during which many wars, invasions and earthquakes have taken place.

" The sacred grove of Asclepios is surrounded by bounds on every side. No men die or women give birth within the enclosure; the same rule is observed in the island of Delos.

" The image of Asclepios is half the size of the image of Olympian Zeus at Athens; it is made of ivory and gold. An inscription sets forth that the sculptor was Thrasymedes, a Parian, son of Arignotos. The god is seated on a throne, grasping a staff, while holding his other hand over the head of the serpent; and a dog, lying by his side, is also represented. On the throne are carved in relief the deeds of Argive heroes: of Bellerophon against the Chimaera, and Perseus cutting off Medusa's head. Over against the temple is the place where the suppliants of the god sleep.

" A round building of white marble, called the Rotunda (Tholos) is near by, worth seeing. There is a picture by Pausias: Eros who has thrown away his bow and arrows, and has picked up a lyre instead. There is also another painting, that, too, a work of Pausias: Drunkenness drinking out of a crystal goblet; and in the picture you can see the crystal goblet and through it the woman's face.

" Tablets stood within the enclosure. Of old there were more of them: in my time six were left. On these tablets are engraved the names of men and women who were healed by Asclepios; together with the disease from which each suffered and how he was cured. Apart from the others, stands an ancient tablet which says that Hippolytos dedicated 20 horses to the god. The people of Aricia tell a tale, that agrees with the inscription on this tablet, that when Hippolytos was done to death by the curses of Theseus, Asclepios raised him from the dead; on coming to life again, Hippolytos . . . went away to Aricia in Italy. There he reigned and consecrated a precinct to Artemis . . .

" In the Epidaurian sanctuary there is a theatre, in my opinion most especially worth seeing. It is true, in splendor the Roman theatres far transcend all the theatres in the world, and in size the theatre at Megalopolis in Arcadia is superior; but for harmony and beauty, what architect could vie with Polyclitos? For it was Polyclitos who made this theatre and the round building also.

" Within the grove is a temple of Artemis and an image of Epione; also a sanctuary of Aphrodite and Themis; and a Stadion formed like most Greek stadions, by banks of earth; also a fountain worth seeing for its roof and general splendor.

" The buildings erected in our time by the Roman senator Antonius include a bath of Asclepios and a sanctuary of the gods whom they name ' bountiful '. Further, he built a temple to Health, as well as to Asclepios and Apollo with the surname ' Egyptians '. There was also a colonnade called the Colonnade of Cotys: after the roof had collapsed, the whole edifice was in ruins . . ., this too he restored. Above the grove is Mount Titthion and another mountain named Kynortion. On the latter is a very ancient sanctuary of Maleatas Apollo . . . "

(Pausanias, Book II, 27:1—7)

Pausanias has not given a complete list of all the constructions which were in the Hieron. As we know from other sources and from the inscriptions found, the buildings belonging to the Hieron of Epidauros during Roman times were approximately the following:

The Propylaea, the Temple of Asclepios, the Tholos or Thymele, Asclepios' Altar, a monumental Fountain, the Abaton or Enkoimitirion, the Temple of Artemis, the Theatre, the Stadion, the Odeion, the Library, the Gymnasium, the Palaestra, the Stoa of Kotys, the " sacred constructions " or priests' habitations, the Temple of Hygieia, the Temple of Themis, the Temple of Aphrodite, the Temple called " Epidoteion " (of Telesphoros, Hypnos, Oniros and Machaon), the Temple of the Egyptian Apollo and Asclepios, the " Katagogion " or Guest House, a vast construction with galleries, Greek and Roman Baths, cisterns, stelae of cures, altars, etc., as well as several unidentified buildings.

The ruins only and the foundations of most of these

buildings remain today. They are, however, very interesting and they fill us with beauty. " I have so long contemplated the beauty, that my gaze is full of it ", sings our Alexandrine poet, Cavafis. The theatre of " harmony and beauty ", as Pausanias says, survived almost intact and dominates the same enchanting site. And of the famous Tholos, of the Temples of Asclepios and Artemis and of the Propylaea, the archaeologists have rescued so many fragments from the entablatures, the ornate ceilings, etc., that it has been possible to make the remarkable reconstructions exhibited in the Museum. It is thus possible to study the richness and the diversity of the ornamental motifs, the ornaments of the ceilings, the capitals, etc.

Apart from these reconstructions, in the Museum of Epidauros some statues and castings of Asclepios, Athena and Aphrodite, of the Amazones and the Nereids, the Stelae of miraculous healings, Isyllos' Hymn, the inscription of Apellas, the surgical instruments, some statues of the Roman period, various offerings, etc. are worth seeing.

The visit of the excavation site is also interesting. The basements and the remnants of the principal buildings have been uncovered, and so, with the help of our topographical map (p. 10), this visit can become very easy and profitable.

THE CURES

The main purpose of the Asclepieion of Epidauros was not, as we saw, therapeutic. It was a spiritual institution of worship, with Tempels, a Theatre, an Odeion, a Stadion, a Gymnasium and a Library, where every pilgrim could purify and regenerate himself.

The healings of the body and mind which occurred there, were the natural and necessary outcome, firstly, of the worship of the " Saviour " Asclepios (the absolute good) and, secondly, of the spiritual rebirth (or " awakening " from sleep and dreaming) which takes place when an individual identifies himself and becomes conscious of his true nature.

The true nature of man was considered to be mainly spiritual. His natural state is a condition of perfect harmony and health, which remains undisturbed as long as it is kept in tune (" think spiritually ") with the divine harmony and order, which governs the universe.

Disease is the unnatural condition caused by something foreign which comes to disturb the reigning harmony. But the resulting inharmony is only temporary. The natural and necessary law is that perfect harmony will be restored again. Because the living god is the god of health, Asclepios, who destroys everything contrary to himself.

This something, however, which tries to disturb our natural harmony is not real, it has no real substance; it is but a " chimera " (a fanciful monster with a lion's head, a goat's body and a serpent's tail), an illusion, a dream.

Let us remember that, according to Pausanias' description, on the throne where the chryselephantine cult statue of Asclepios was seated, in his magnificent Temple, the figures in relief represented the hero Bellerophon killing the " Chimera " and Perseus cutting off the head of the Medusa (another monster, which had snakes for hair and turned anyone into stone who looked upon it).

Though fantastic, however, these enemies of our natural harmony are very dangerous, because they assail our mind and our thinking, and they create a lot of conscious or unconscious fears or phobias and terrible passions. If they are not controlled in time, they can strangle us, like the Lernea Hydra. First, they attack a man mentally, and if they find that he is unguarded or spiritually too weak to behead them immediately, they settle in his mind and from there they spread to incapacitate also his body.

It is the mind that governs the body; it is our thought which is the main factor in the formation of our organism. Starting from this fundamental premise, the ancient Greeks had searched and studied deeply the interrelation which exists between these two elements. And they had concluded that if the disease is not allowed to pass, consciously or unconsciously, through the mind, it cannot reach the body.

"Νοῦς ὁρᾷ καί νοῦς ἀκούει · τ'ἄλλα τυφλά καί κωφά".
" It is the mind that sees and hears, the rest is deaf and blind ", the famous (though quite unknown to us) tragedian Epicharmos summarized epigrammatically. (Let us remember the high esteem Plato had for this prominent writer of the beginning of the 5th century B. C.; as Diogenes Laertius relates, the great philosopher kept Epicharmos' works under his pillow! He wrote more than 35 dramas, which, as we know from his contemporaries, were full of profound philosophical and metaphysical ideas, but unfortunately none was preserved. Obviously they must have been of such high quality, the works which were represented at the Theatre of Epidauros, works proclaiming truths that healed and freed from materiality.)

Considering thus that the cause of every disease is mainly mental, the method to cure it should also be mental or spiritual. The patient who, failing to guard his mind, has let himself become sick (either because he did not know how to protect himself, or owing to the lessening of his spiritual resistance, or because of his little faith in the divine) will be healed at the Asclepieion, where the high spirituality of the priests and the profoundly religious, spiritual and artistic atmosphere of the place will certainly help him to cast out all his erroneous beliefs and illusions and so recover his natural and harmonious condition.

A radical healing is thus obtained only when the mind itself is cured; when there is a change of mind (METANOIA). For together with the mind, the body also is necessarily healed. The body can, of course, be also cured directly, with various materia medica, but this cure is only temporary. As the generative cause of the disease dwelling in the mind has not been eliminated, it may, at any time, call forth new disharmonies in other parts of the body.

In ancient Greece, both the above methods of healing recognized Asclepios as their god and protector, because, as we saw, he himself had used both these me-

Apellas' inscription on his cure

thods, though he evidently much preferred the spiritual one. This first method was followed chiefly by the initiated priests of Asclepios, those powerful thinkers of a higher spirituality, who, using exclusively spiritual means, reached quite amazing results in the Asclepieion of Epidauros. The second method was followed by the Asclepiades, those practical or lay physicians, who developed their science independently of the priesthood of Asclepios, and attained also, with the " Father of Medicine ", Hippocrates, and other outstanding scientists, remarkable results, though, of course, not comparable to the wonderful achievements of our modern medical science.

As we have seen, even in the Asclepieion of Epidauros, but mainly during the later years of the Roman occupation, some therapeutic means were used which were not exclusively spiritual, like hot baths, dietetics, hygienic treatments, etc. A good example of this blending of the two methods can be seen on the marble stele dedicated by Apellas, the scholar from Asia Minor, during the 2nd half of the 2nd century A. D., and which is now exhibited in the Museum of Epidauros.

*

The two marble stelae of cures, which are shown in the Museum of Epidauros constitute a part of the official record of the activity of the Asclepieion during the first two centuries of its operation (from the end of the 6th to the end of the 4th century B. C.). They have been inscribed by the priesthood and they relate 43 healings, chosen among thousands which occurred there. As we know from Pausanias and from some inscriptions, there were many other tablets of healings in the Hieron, which have not been preserved.

The cases recorded are absolutely authentic and truthful, though some of them should be understood symbolically. The great contemporary writer Henry Miller, who has written some extremely interesting pages about Epidauros in his book " the Colossus of Maroussi " says: " There is no mystery in my mind as to the nature of the cures which were wrought at this great therapeutic centre of the ancient world. Here the healer himself was healed, first and most important step in the development of the art, which is not medical but religious. "

The first stele begins with the inscription:

"ΘΕΟΣ ΤΥΧΑ ΑΓΑΘΑ"   " GOD. GOOD FORTUNE! "

" Cures of Apollo and Asclepios "

and relates the first case as follows:

" Cleo was with child for five years. After she had been pregnant for five years she came as a suppliant to the god and slept in the Abaton. As soon as she left it and got outside the temple precincts, she bore a son who, immediately after birth, washed himself at the fountain and walked about with his mother. In return for this favor she inscribed on her offering: ' Admirable is not the greatness of the tablet, but the divine power. Cleo carried the burden in her womb for five years, until she slept in the Abaton and the god healed her '." (Stele I, lines 3—9).

From the first case it is made very clear that the only means used for this healing was the " admirable divine power ", the same power which will be, as we shall see, utilized, as the sole therapeutic agent, in all the 43 cases preserved. No allusion whatever is made to any remedy or other material means. The illness which had assailed Cleo's mind was but an illusion, as every disease is; it made her, however, suffer for more than five years, till she came to the Asclepieion and was cured.

For everything, the second case tells us, we must seek god's help; not with generalities, but with specific petitions and a deep conviction that we are going to obtain what we sincerely desire, for everything is possible to god.

" A woman of Pellene came to the Temple to ask God to grant her a child. Having slept in the Abaton she saw a vision. It seemed to her that she asked the god that she might get pregnant and that if she asked for something else he would grant her that too, but she answered she did not need anything else. When she had become pregnant, she carried in her womb for three years, until she came again to the Hieron and supplicated the god concerning the birth. When she had fallen asleep, she saw a vision. It seemed to her that the god asked her if she had not obtained all she had asked for and was pregnant; about the birth she had added nothing, and that, although he had asked if she needed anything else, she should say so and he would grant her this too. But since now she had come for this as a suppliant to him, he said he would accord even it to her. After that, she hastened to leave the Abaton, and when she was outside the sacred precincts, she gave birth to a girl! " (Stele I, lines 9—22).

For those who do not have a sufficient knowledge of the greatness of the true god and of his omnipotence and who, though they have faith (since they come as suppliants), they still have some doubt about god's capacity to cure even diseases which, to our human sense, may seem incurable, the following case is related:

" A woman from Athens called Ambrosia was blind in one eye. She came as a suppliant to the god. As she walked about in the Temple, she laughed at some of the cures as incredible and impossible, that the lame and the blind should be healed by merely having a dream. In her sleep she had a vision. It seemed to her that the god stood by her and said that he would cure her, but that in payment he would ask her to dedicate to the Temple a silver pig as a memorial of her foolishness. After saying this, he cut the diseased eyeball and poured in some drug. When day came, she walked out of the Abaton completely sound. " (Stele I, lines 33—41).

Let us watch lest we are also asked to offer a silver pig to the god for our lack of spirituality and our obstinacy in remaining materialists, when the supremacy of the spirit is so evident!

The fact that the spirit has the power to heal even from afar, when the patient is absent, is illustrated by the following case:

" Arata, a woman of Lacedaemon was dropsical. Her mother left her in Lacedaemon and came to Epidauros to beg god to cure her daughter. She slept in the Temple and saw the following dream: It seemed to her that the god cut off her daughter's head and hung up her body in such a way that her throat was turned downwards. Out of it came a huge quantity of fluid matter. Then he took down the body and fitted the head back on to the neck. After she had seen this dream she went back to Lacedaemon where she found her daughter in good health; she had seen the same dream " (Stele II, l. 1—6). Obviously these women, in spite of their deep faith in god, had but a dim idea of the divine possibilities. Their candid dreams reveal that they did not know that the spirit acts instantaneously, without the use of any material means, like surgical operations, etc.

The spirit, on the other hand, has dominion even over inanimate things. And as it has the power to heal men, it can also restore a broken vase! This fact is demonstrated by the following case showing also the great kindness of Asclepios towards a poor servant who had a deep faith in his omnipotence:

" A slave bearing various vases was going to the Temple, when he fell near the tenstadia stone. When he had got up he opened his bag and looked at the broken vessels. When he saw that the goblet from which his master was accustomed to drink was also broken, he was in great distress and sat down to try to fit the pieces together again. But a passer-by saw him and said: ' Foolish fellow, why do you put the goblet together in vain? For this one not even Asclepios of Epidauros could put to rights again '. The boy, hearing this, put the pieces back in the bag and went on to the Temple. When he got there he opened the bag and brought the goblet out of it, and it was entirely whole; and he related to his master what had happened and had been said. When the master heard that, he dedicated the goblet to the god. " (Stele I, lines 79—89).

The following case shows that if the healing is limited only to the body of the patient and he does not become more spiritual, more honest and unselfish, there will be a relapse:

" Hermon of Thassos being blind, his blindness was cured by Asclepios. But, since afterwards he did not bring the thank-offerings, the god made him blind again. When he came back and slept in the Abaton, the god made him well again. " (Stele II, lines 7—9).

There were some (even Pindar) who have censured the priests of Asclepios for their supposed greediness, because they asked from those who had been healed to show their gratitude by bringing ' thank-offerings ' to the Hieron, according to their economic situation: the wealthy a great deal, the poor little or nothing. This reproach seems to us entirely unfounded we know that the offerings were not destined for the priests, but were used for the erection of the splendid artistic monuments we can still admire today and which served to increase the spiritual radiance of the shrine and, consequently, its healing efficacy too.

As we can read on a stele exhibited in the Museum of Epidauros, the priests kept very detailed accounts of all their expenses for the construction of the edifices of the Hieron. (This inscription itemizes especially the expenses made for the erection of Asclepios' Temple and the Tholos).

The loving-kindness and the great unselfishness of the god are demonstrated by the following instance:
" A boy of Epidauros named Euphanes was suffering from stone. He slept in the Abaton. It seemed to him that the god stood by him and asked: ' What will you give me if I cure you? ' ' Ten dice ', he answered. The god laughed and said to him that he would cure him. When day came, he walked out sound. " (Stele I, l. 68-71).
In all the cases recorded, Asclepios, smiling, compassionate and full of kindness, appears in the dreams of his suppliants and, as soon as they beseech him, " before daybreak ", they are already healed. He has the power and the willingness to accomplish everything, without the use of any material means.

This, however, was happening in the 5th and 4th centuries B. C. and we do not know for how many centuries more. But, at the end of the 2nd century A. D. the situation had completely changed. The ancient spiritual centre had taken the appearance of a watering resort and had been invaded by temples of foreign and secondary gods. The pilgrims still have faith in Asclepios, but as to a physician who gives them remedies and good hygienic advices. They remain for months in the Asclepieion, they read in the Library, they take baths, they go to the theatre ... And the strangest thing is that when they leave they are sound and content. " Healed and full of gratitude I departed from the Hieron ", says Apellas, the scholar from Asia Minor, who dedicated to Asclepios a stele now displayed in the Museum.

We give the beginning only of this long inscription, which continues with a lot of other diseases and the prescriptions and counsels received from the god (headaches, blisters, inflammations, tonsils, etc.).

" In the priesthood of Poplius Aelius Antiochus ".
" I, Marcus Julius Apellas, from Mylasa of Karia, falling often into sickness and suffering from dyspepsia, came to Epidauros sent by the god himself. In the course of my journey, in Aegina, the god told me not to be so irritable. When I arrived at the temple, he told me for two days to keep my head covered, and for these two days it rained; to eat cheese and bread, celery with lettuce, to wash myself without help, to practise running, to take lemon peel, to soak it in water; near the spot of the Akoai in the bath to press against the wall; to take a walk in the upper portico, to take some passive exercise, to sprinkle myself with sand, to walk around barefoot in the bathroom, before plunging into the hot water, to pour wine over myself, to bathe without help and to give an Attic drachma to the bath attendant, to offer sacrifice in common to Asclepios, Epione and the Eleusinian goddesses, to take milk with honey. When one day I had drunk milk alone he said: " Put honey in the milk so ' that it can get through ' ... "

But let us return to the first, and certainly the most interesting, centuries of the long history of the Asclepieion of Epidauros, which lasted about a millenium, in order to examine, on the basis of the available documents, the procedure followed for the cures.

In the aforementioned cases we have seen that the patient slept in the Abaton, had a dream and when he woke up he was already healed. This sleeping in the Abaton was called " ENKOIMISIS ".

It seems so simple and childlike that some (among them even Aristophanes) misunderstood it and they concluded that the ancient Greeks must have been very naïve and credulous people to give faith to such tales. Others have advanced the supposition that the priests were using some tricks or even medicines, which they did not reveal in order to strengthen the faith of the people in the god and so be able to compete with the secular physicians!

The careful study of the inscriptions proves that the ENKOIMISIS was not the basic and always necessary means for the cures. It was the culminating or last phase of a long series of purifications, which contributed to exalt the patient's faith and to spiritualize his thought so as to make him receptive, directly or through the medium of the priests, to the divine healing power.

We know very little indeed about these preliminary purificatory ceremonies, which certainly played a fundamental role in the healings. We do not even know how long they lasted.

In the first stele of cures we read that a voiceless child came with his father as a suppliant to the Hieron and was healed, in the presence of the " pyrophoros " (the priest's assistant) before the final stage of the ENKOI-MISIS, " as soon as he had performed the preliminary sacrifices and fulfilled the usual rites " (Stele I, lines 41—48, partially damaged).

The sacrifices and the rites to be fulfilled were ordained by the priests, who were the highest religious authority in the Asclepieion and were helped by various assistants. At the Hieron of Epidauros the following officials served hierarchically under the priest: the " NAKO-ROS " (priestess), the " PYROPHOROS " (the priest's assistant " who bears the fire "), the " ZAKOROS " (woman assisting the priestess), the " NAOPHYLAKES " (the temple's guardians), the " HIEROMNIMONES " (" those keeping in mind the sacred words "), the " AOIDOI " (the cantors). And there were also cooks, servants, flute players, etc.

The priests, with their assistants, followed the development of the pilgrims' diseases and, according to each case, they decided either to prolong the preliminary ceremonies or to admit them to the final stage of the ENKOIMISIS. We do not know much about these preliminary ceremonies, not even in which place they took place. As if the radiance of the god and the spirituality of the shrine were not sufficient to explain the cures, some writers have alluded to secret incantations and mysterious rituals which supposedly took place in the " ADYTON " (the " holy of holies ") of the Abaton or in the subterranean part of the Tholos. But all these are pure hypotheses, contradicted by the official inscriptions.

An inscription on Stele I (lines 90—94) refers to a curious person who wanted to know what was happening within the Abaton:

" A man named Aeschines, when the suppliants were already asleep, climbed up a tree and tried to see over into the Abaton. But he fell from the tree on to some fencing and his eyes were injured. In a pitiable state of blindness, he came as a suppliant to the god and slept in the Abaton and was healed. "

*

The only thing we know for certain is that a very close and ancient link existed between the Asclepieia of Epidauros, the Eleusinian Mysteries and the Oracle of Delphi. In the Hieron of Epidauros a special temple had been erected for the worship of the Eleusinian goddesses Demeter (under the name of Penteleke) and Persephone; the Eleusinian Mysteries, on the other hand, had consecrated to Asclepios a day of the Great Eleusinians, called " Epidauria ". Besides, the Oracle of Delphi was always supporting the Asclepieion of Epidauros. Many times, when after an epidemic, delegations of Greek cities addressed themselves to Apollo, his Oracle referred them to Asclepios of Epidauros and advised them to establish an Asclepieion in their own city.

And the Epidaurian poet Isyllos had to get, as we have seen, the authorization of Delphi's oracle in order to erect within the sacred precinct of Epidauros the stele of his famous hymn proclaiming that Epidauros was the birth-place of Asclepios. Furthermore, in some inscriptions and votive offerings, Asclepios is named " MYSTIS " (the initiated) and his priests, ordinarily called " the priests of the Saviour Asclepios " or simply " of the Saviour ", are sometimes designated as " the torch bearers of the Eleusinian Mysteries " or " HIEROPHAN-TES ".

During the first centuries, the priests of the Asclepieion of Epidauros were not irremovable, as they became later, in Roman times. They were elected for one year, but they could be reelected and remain in service for a second or a third year (as mentioned in some inscriptions) and probably even for longer periods. They had no medical knowledge and were not chosen among all the inhabitants of the city, but exclusively from certain families known for their high spirituality. These families kept jealously and transmitted from generation to generation the sacred traditions of the Hieron and its secret rites. To be eligible for the post of priest, the candidate should already have served in one or more of the subsidiary posts, in order to have the required experience.

The priests of Epidauros were very well remunerated. Their income allowed them to live with dignity and to dedicate themselves entirely to their high mission. Contrary to the other Asclepieia, they did not take any part of the offerings, which were distributed to the inferior officers only. Furthermore, the most usual offering to Asclepios was but a cock!

The priesthood lived within the sacred precinct in comfortable habitations, built especially for them. Such dwellings for the priests were also found near the Temple of Apollo Maleatas, on Mount Kynortion.

During the preparatory period of purification, the suppliant wandered freely in the sacred grove, which, as we have seen, was open from all sides. He could thus read and ponder over the official inscriptions of miraculous cures and the private votive tablets proclaiming the omnipotence and the loving-kindness of the god. He could also see the theatrical representations of tragedies and comedies, which expressed profound moral thoughts and powerful metaphysical verities. He could also assist at musical concerts, rhythmic dances and athletic games, study the works of the best writers in the public Library and fill his thought with the artistic beauty and the harmony of the masterpieces all around him.

Even the Temple of Asclepios, the famous Temple with the chryselephantine cult statue of the god, was always open, day and night. This was quite unusual in the ancient world. The temples then opened their doors to the public during their official feasts only, except for the Asclepieia, which held daily services to praise and glorify Asclepios. The Temple was always full of suppliants and from daybreak " matins ", hymns and paeans were sung, accompagnied by professional cantors, who were members of the priesthood.

Poetry, as Plato says, is the best means of glorifying and propitiating god, because it is a " mania sent by the gods "; the poet becoming " EKPHRON " (out of himself) and " ENTHEOS " (in god), can understand the deity and glorify it appropriately.

The paean was at first a hymn sung in honour of Apollo and Artemis for the appeasement of epidemics (as in the 1st Rhapsody of the Iliad, v. 472); later, however, it became the most appropriate hymn to praise Asclepios. As the famous paean of Sophocles, which for centuries was sung in the Asclepieia, has not been preserved, we give below another hymn to Asclepios inscribed on a marble stele found in the outskirts of Athens, dating from the 4th century B. C. (this stele is now exhibited in the Museum of Kassel, in Germany):

Arise Asclepios, lord of men and healer,
Gentle-minded child of god Apollo and noble Coronis,
Dispersing sleep from your eyes, heed the prayers of
Your worshippers who, rejoicing greatly,
Propitiate your prime power, health, gentle-minded As-
Arise and be pleased to give ear to your hymn, [clepios.
You whom we invoke with the cry: " Hail ".

All these preparatory means for the purification and the spiritualization of the pilgrim's thought had the effect of healing him, without being always necessary to resort to the last stage of the ENKOIMISIS. This is confirmed by the fact that of the 43 cases of cures recorded in the two stelae preserved, 8 healings were effected without ENKOIMISIS (cases 5, 10, 16 and 20 of the 1st stele and 21, 25, 26 and 43 of the 2nd stele). In one case, the healing occurred while the patient remained home at Lacedaemon (Sparta) and it was here mother who went to sleep in the Abaton.

Therefore, we think it is not in the ENKOIMISIS that the secret of the miraculous cures of the Asclepieion of Epidauros should be sought, but rather in the tremendous spiritual power of the divine and in the reflection of its healing power, which the priests of Asclepios knew how to practise and use, owing to their superior spirituality and their close communion with the divine source. (Let us remember that the priests of Delphi were called saints and prophets). And furthermore, in the spiritual and therapeutic radiance sent out by this supremely artistic, harmonious and spiritual centre, which had the effect of exalting and spiritualizing the pilgrims' deep faith in the divine and make them receptive to its healing and regenerating power.

Sanctuary of Asclepios
The main buildings

1 Temple of Asclepios — 2 Tholos (Rotunda) — 3 Abaton or Enkoimeterion — 4 Ancient Abaton (?) —
5 Temple of Artemis — 6 Great Altar of Asclepios — 7 Sacred Fountain

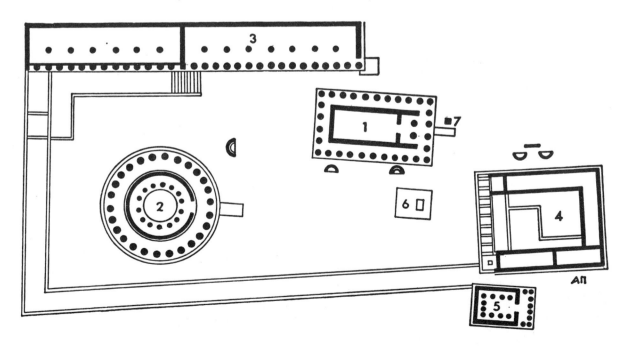

Reconstruction of the temple of Asclepios

THE REVIVAL OF EPIDAUROS, FESTIVALS

Since 1954 Epidauros has taken on new life.

In the famous theatre of Polycleitos, " full of harmony and beauty ", the tragedies and comedies of the most renowned of the ancient dramatists are again presented every summer, from June to August. Organized by the National Theatre of Greece, with the collaboration of the National Organisation of Tourism and the Club " Periigitiki ", these representations have been officially established as the " Festival of Epidauros " or " Epidauria ".

These presentations were soon followed by the Lyric Scene, which performed operas, with the participation of Greek and foreign artists of world renown. Dimitri Mitropoulo composed the music of Hippolytos, with which the festival was inaugurated (his statue was erected near the theatre) and Maria Callas sang the Norma of Bellini.

The success was immediate. The Festivals of Epidauros were soon recognized as an international event. More than 100,000 spectators follow them every summer.

The sanctuary of Epidauros, the most famous of the Temples of Asclepios, the god of Socrates, has preserved, although in ruins, all its spirituality and beauty of old. The modern tourist is impressed. " At Epidauros, in the stillness, in the great peace that came over me, I heard the heart of the world beat ". (H. Miller).

DESCRIPTION OF THE PRINCIPAL MONUMENTS OF EPIDAUROS

1. THE PROPYLAEA (illustration p. 32)

The official entrance to the sanctuary was from the north, where was the terminal of the two, 17.50 metres wide, roads coming from Epidauros on the sea and from Argos. The precinct was not enclosed; it was only surrounded by bounds.

The majestic Propylaea were erected in the 4th c. B. C., after the construction of Asclepios'Temple, the Tholos and the Theatre. Built in tufa, they were 20 metres in breadth and had in front six marble columns of the Ionic order and six of the Corinthian order on the inner side. The gargoyles represented lion's heads, like those of the Tholos and Asclepios' Temple.

The following rhythmed inscription was carved on the architrave:

> " Pure must be he who enters the fragrant temple;
> Purity means to think nothing but holy thoughts ".

A reconstruction of the entablature of the Propylaea may be seen in the Museum of Epidauros. On the excavation site the foundations only and some remnants remain.

Cross section through the interior of the temple of Asclepios (Reconstruction)

2. ASCLEPIOS' TEMPLE (ill. p. 37, 40, 48)

A majestic monument which contained the chryselephantine cult statue of the god Asclepios', the work of the sculptor Thrasymedes of Paros. The image of the god in gigantic size was seated on a throne; he was grasping in one hand a staff with a serpent coiled around it and holding the other over the head of a dragon. A dog was represented crouching by his side. On one side of the throne, which was also made of gold and ivory, were in relief representations of the hero Bellerophon killing the Chimera (a fire breathing monster with a lion's head, a goat's body and a serpent's tail) and Perseus beheading the Medusa (another monster with snakes for hair and a gaze that turned into stone anyone who looked at her.)

The Temple was in the Doric order, peripteral, 24.50 metres long and 13.22 m. wide. It was divided into a pronaos and a cella (sekos), without an opisthodomos. The colonnade which surrounded it had 6 columns at the front and back and 11 columns on each side, 5.20 metres high. It was built in tufa, stuccoed and painted in white. The capitals and the entablature had many multicolored ornaments. The marble gargoyles were also colored and represented lion's heads. The roof of cypress and pine wood was covered with tiles. On the " acroteria " were statues representing Nereids and winged Victories. The sculptures on the southern pediment of the façade represented battles of Centaurs and on the western pediment battles of Amazons.

The floor of the Temple was paved with black and white plates; its ceiling was ornamented with various decorations (golden stars, floral motifs, etc.). The ornaments of the wooden door of the sekos were in gold and ivory and were fixed with golden nails.

The Temple was built in about 380 B. C., under the general supervision of the architect Theodotos, who together with Skopas constructed the famous Mausoleum of Halicarnassus (one of the seven wonders of the ancient world). Apart from the chryselephantine statue of Asclepios, Thrasymedes executed the carved decorations of the ceiling and the ornaments of the door. The beautiful sculptures of the pediments (ill. p. 52) and the Nereids and winged Victories of the acroteria (ill. p. 50, 51, 53) were executed by Timotheos, one of the greatest artists of the 4th century B. C. Under Timotheos' direction many other known artists worked, like Hectoride, Agathinos and Lysias.

From an inscription we know that the Temple took 4 years and 8 months to build and cost about 100,000 drachme. In Epidauros' Museum there is a partial reconstruction of Asclepios' Temple with its marvelous ornamentation. On the excavation site the foundations and some remnants only are left.

3. THOLOS (ROTUNDA) OR THYMELE (ill. p. 55—67)

Built between 370 and 330 B. C. by Polycleitos the Younger, who also constructed the Theatre, this Tholos was considered one of the most perfect and gracious monuments of ancient Greece.

Round in form, the Tholos was surrounded externally by a colonnade of 21,76 metres in diametre, consisting of 26 Doric columns, in tufa, stuccoed and painted in white. Behind these columns was the circular wall of the sekos, decorated with

19

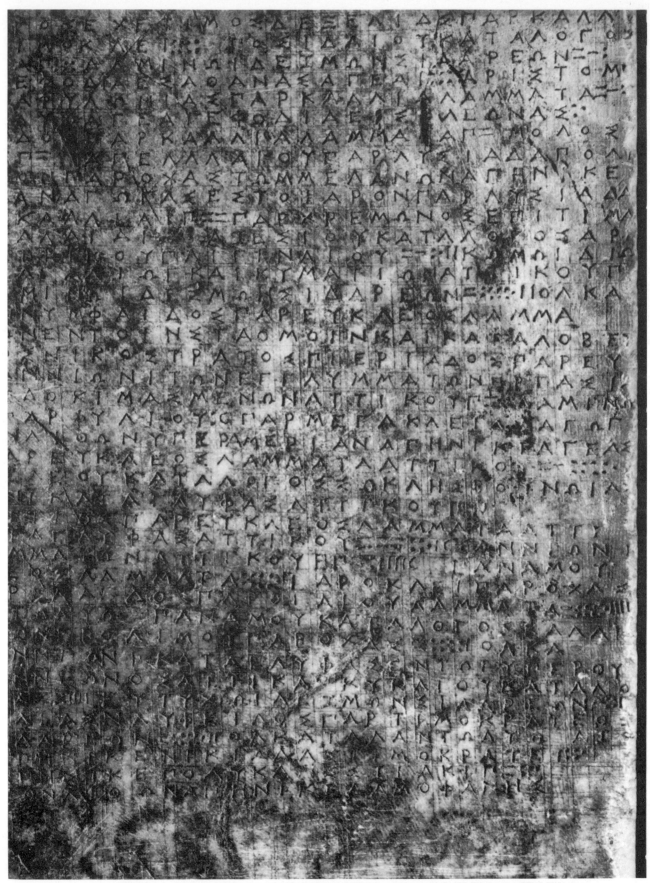

Inscription of expenses for the construction of Asklepios' Temple and the Tholos (detail)

many polychrome ornaments and paintings by the famous painter Pausias. Pausanias depicts two of them: one representing EROS, who has thrown away his bow and arrows and has picked up a lyre instead and the other showing METHE (drunkenness) drinking out of a crystal goblet. Behind the wall of the sekos was a circular colonnade of 14 marble columns with beautiful Corinthian capitals. The ceiling was coffered and magnificently painted. The pavement was in black and white marble.

Under the Tholos was a mysterious construction forming a labyrinth, with 3 convergent walls still in fairly good preservation. The purpose of the Tholos, called also Thymele (altar) in many inscriptions, was never revealed. According to some suppositions, it was used for the official banquets of the priests and the archontes, or for some religious or ritualistic ceremonies, for dramatic or musical contests, or even as a treasury, etc. The most probable hypothesis, however, is that in this subterranean labyrinth was he tomb of the chthonian hero Asclepios, symbolized by a snake. Thus the heroic nature of Asclepios was honored secretly in the Tholos, while his divine nature was publicly worshipped in the nearby Temple.

4. THE ABATON (dormitory, ill. p. 34, 35, 36)

To the North of the Tholos, near the Temple of Asclepios, was the Abaton or " ENKOIMITIRION " (dormitory) where the suppliants slept in order to see the god in their dream and be healed. The word Abaton means that its entrance was forbidden to the non-initiated and to those who had not completed the preliminary ceremonies of purification, which were necessary for the appearance of the god.

The Abaton, built partly in two stories, was 70 metres long and 9.50 metres wide, with a long colonnade on the side of the Tholos and the Temple. It was constructed in tufa and formed two adjacent stoas, closed by a wall on the north side. Its eastern part dates from the 4th century B. C., while its two-storied extension to the west was erected in the 3rd century.

In the N. E. corner of the Abaton was the sacred Fountain, mentioned by Pausanias as " worth seeing ". The tablets recording the miraculous healings, now exhibited in the Museum, were found in the ruins of the Abaton.

5. THE TEMPLE OF ARTEMIS (ill. p. 38, 54)

This Temple dates from the 4th century B. C. and was built in tufa. It was in the Doric order, 13.30 metres long and 9.40 metres wide. In its eastern façade it had a row of six Doric columns; but there were no columns on its other external sides. In the interior there was a colonnade of 10 columns in tufa. The roof and the gargoyles were of marble. Three statues of the acroteria, representing winged Victories, were found in its ruins. This temple was considered as the most beautiful of the Hieron, after Asclepios' Temple.

6. THE THEATRE (ill. covers and p. 28, 68, 70—79)

The theatre dates from the middle of the 4th century B. C. and was constructed by the architect Polycleitos the Younger, who also erected the Tholos. It was considered as the most beautiful of all the theatres of ancient Greece. Remarkable, as Pausanias reported, for its " harmony and beauty ", this theatre was fortunately preserved almost intact.

It is situated outside the sacred precinct, on the slopes of Mount Kynortion, in a site with exceptionally good acoustics. Its seats, cut in the rock, were oriented towards the North, so that the spectators could contemplate in front of them all the monuments of the Hieron and the magnificent landscape of wooded mountains all around.

The theatre had room for approximately 14,000 spectators. It was built in white limestone, except for the stage and the lateral retaining walls which were in tufa. The auditorium, in the form of a segment of a circle greater than a semi-circle, has 55 rows of seats divided in zones by a horizontal passage called " diazoma ". The lower zone has 34 rows and the upper zone 21. Vertically the seats are divided by 13 flights of stairs, into 12 tiers called " kerkides " in the lower zone and 22 in the upper zone.

The orchestra forms a complete circle, 20.30 metres in diameter. In its centre is the round base of the Thymele (altar). The stage was 26.15 metres long and 6 metres wide, two storied and 3.50 metres high. The construction in front of the scene was called the proscenium; on either side of it were wings called " parascenia ", where the actors dressed. Today only the foundations of the stage can be seen.

Two monumental double doorways, called " Parodoi ", with pilasters embellished with Corinthian capitals, gave access to the theatre. They were in tufa and they have been restored recently.

In spite of its great size, the theatre is perfectly harmonious and its accoustics are exceptional. Its restoration has been completed and since 1954 a Festival is organized there every summer, during the months of June to August, with representations of ancient drama and other performances, which attract many visitors.

7. THE GYMNASIUM AND THE ODEION (ill. p. 43, 44)

The Gymnasium was built about the end of the 4th or the beginning of the 3rd century B. C. Its entrance (or Propylaea) formed a colonnade in the Doric order. This huge construction (75.57 metres long and 69.53 metres wide) had an interior court, surrounded by a colonnade of 16 columns and many rooms, exedrae and halls. Lectures and discussions on rhetoric and philosophy took place in these halls, while the young athletes exercised themselves under the galleries and in the court.

During the Roman period, an Odeion was built in the interior of the Gymnasium, and the Propylaea were transformed into a Temple of Hygieia. In fairly good preservation, the remnants of these constructions may be seen in the excavation site.

8. THE XENON (HOTEL) OR KATAGOGION (ill. p. 45)

This was the biggest construction of Epidauros and was built on the S. E. part of the Hieron, towards the theatre. It served as a Guest House for the numerous visitors who came to the sanctuary.

It had the form of a square, each side of which was 76 metres long. It was divided into 4 blocks and comprised 160 rooms, which encircled a central court. Most probably it was two-storied.

9. THE STADION (ill. p. 80)

Built since the 5th century B. C., it was rectangular in shape, 196.45 metres long (the distance of a stadium) and 23.30 metres wide. From the beginning of the 5th century B. C., gymnic games (foot races, jumps, wrestling, discus, boxing, etc.) and musical contests were organized in this Stadion.

The spectators were seated on the ground along the longer sides of the course, but there were also some stone stalls for the umpires and the officials, as well as private seats on which the donators had their names inscribed. To the North there was a subterranean gallery (" krypte ") uniting the Stadion with the Hieron. The officials and the athletes, starting from Asclepios' Temple, came through this gallery in procession to the Stadion for the official inauguration of the games.

Before the construction of the theatre, the musical and drama competitions were organized in this Stadion.

10. THE SANCTUARY OF APOLLO MALEATAS

Above the theatre on the slopes of Mount Kynortion is the Sanctuary of Apollo Maleatas. The last excavations have revealed that this had been a cult place since the Mycenaean period. The Asclepieion of Epidauros was very closely linked with this much older sanctuary of Apollo Maleatas. The suppliants of Asclepios were asked to offer a preliminary sacrifice on the altar of Apollo Maleatas in his shrine. The surname Maleatas indicates that together with Apollo the local (chthonios) hero Maleatas or Malos, who was also renowned for his therapeutic capacities, was worshipped there.

The Tholos (Reconstruction)

THE MUSEUM OF EPIDAUROS

(Illustr. p. 46—55 and 58—67)

The Museum is situated between the theatre and the entrance leading to the Sanctuary of Asclepios. At the Museum's entrance, on both sides, two corinthian columns of the Tholos and two ionian columns of the Abaton have been erected.

R o o m I. In the first hall, one remarks many stelae covered with inscriptions. These are the official stelae on which were engraved various cases of miraculous cures, extensively narrated in the text, the stele of Isyllos relating the history of Asclepios, Apellas' inscription (cf. text), as well as a big stele with engravings about the expenses incurred for the construction of Asclepios' Temple and of the Tholos.

Medical instruments and various small objects and oil lamps are exhibited in a cupboard (vitrine).

R o o m I I. This room contains plaster casts of statues (Asclepios) and plaster offerings, whose marble originals were found in the excavations of the Sanctuary and are now exhibited in the National Museum of Athens, Epidauros' room (Photos pages 46, 49—53). At the rear of the hall there is a reconstruction of the entablature from a part of the Big Propylaea.

R o o m I I I. In this hall, at the right side, is the partial restoration of one side of Asclepios' Temple (photo 48) — cf. description of the Temple — and, by its side, the restoration of one part of the Temple of Artemis, with gargoyles representing the heads of dogs and wild boars, and acroteria of the pediment (photo 54). In front, at the left side of the hall, one can see those same Victories of the Temple, as well as pieces of statues of various dimensions, which were found during the excavations.

In the middle of the hall, there is a restoration of many

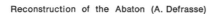

Reconstruction of the Abaton (A. Defrasse)

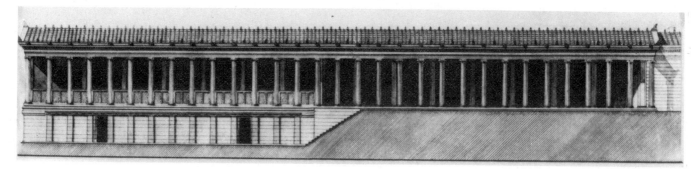

sculptural parts of the Tholos, the Rotunda, described above. At right, the entrance door ornated with rosettes (photo 55) and the coffers of the ceiling of the Tholos. The lilies adorned the ceiling of the outer doric colonnade and the beautiful rosettes ornamented the inner corinthian colonnade (photos 60, 61, 64 and 65).

At left, there is a section of the Tholos, constituting the reconstruction of a part of the outer doric colonnade and of the inner corinthian colonnade, with their respective entablatures and their ceilings with coffers (photos 58, 59, 62 and 63).

At last, there is a fragment of the pavement of the Tholos in black and white marble. At the rear of the hall, on the left side, one can admire a corinthian capital of the Tholos (photos 66 and 67), which was created, as it is believed, by Polycleitos the Younger, the architect of the Tholos and of the Theatre of Epidauros.

BIBLIOGRAPHY

Pausanias: Description of Hellas, " Periigisis ", Book II, Korinthiaka. — P. Cavvadias: Asclepios' Hiéron at Epidauros, Athens 1900 (in Greek). — P. Cavvadias: Les fouilles d'Épidaure, Athens 1891. — Defrasse et Lechat: Épidaure, Paris 1896. — Henri Lechat: Les édifices d'Épidaure, Paris 1896. — Willamovitz: Isyllos von Epidauros. — W. Christ: Das Theater des Polyklet in Epidauros, München 1894. — Chr. Blinkenberg: Epidaurische Weihgeschenke. Kopenhagen, 1897. — Er. Wagner: Ein Besuch in dem Heiligtum des Asklepios zu Epidauros, Wehlau 1907. — Sal. Reinach: La seconde des Stèles des guérisons miraculeuses d'Épidaure, Leroux, Paris, 1885. — S. Herrlich: Epidauros, eine antike Heilstätte, Berlin 1898. — A. Arabantinos: Asclepios and Asclepieia, Athens, 1907 (in Greek). — F. Robert: Épidaure, Édition " Les Belles Lettres ", Paris, 1935. — R. Robert: Thymele, Paris, 1944. — E. J. and L. Edelstein: Asclepius, J. H. Univ. Baltimore USA, 2 Vol., 1945.

Plan of the Theatre (A. Defrasse)

The initials NMA after the numbers of illustrations indicate that these objects are exhibited in the National Museum of Athens

WAYS TO EPIDAUROS

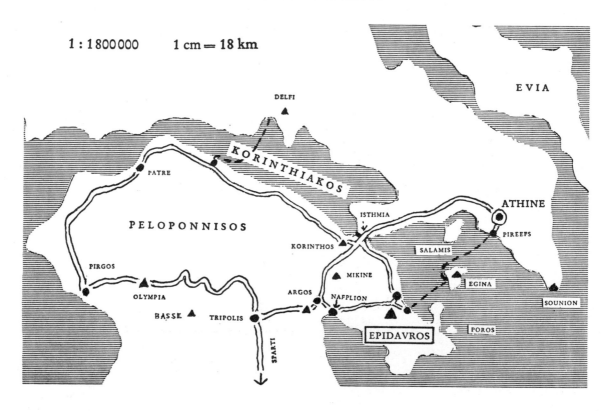

25 NMA
Asclepios
Asclépios
Asklepios

◁   ◁   ◁

26/27
General view of the
Sanctuary from
mount Titthion
Vue générale du
Sanctuaire du haut
du mont Titthion
Blick über den Heili-
gen Bezirk vom
Berg Titthion aus

◁   ◁

28/29
The Theatre
Le Théâtre
Das Theater

The Propylaea of the Sanctuary
es Propylées du Sanctuaire
ie Propyläen des Heiligtums

30/31

The Sanctuary of Asclepios
Le Sanctuaire d'Asclépios
◁ ◁ Das Heiligtum des Asklepios

The Sanctuary of Asclepios
Le Sanctuaire d'Asclépios
Das Heiligtum des Asklepios

The Abaton or Enkoimeterion
L'Abaton ou Enkoimétérion
Das Abaton oder Enkoimeterion

The Abaton or Enkoimeterion
L'Abaton ou Enkoimétérion
Das Abaton oder Enkoimeterion

36
The Abaton or Enkoimeterion
L'Abaton ou Enkoimétérion
Das Abaton oder Enkoimeterion

37
Foundations of Asclepios' Temple
Fondations du Temple d'Asclépios
Fundamente des Asklepiostempels

The Temple of Artemis
Le Temple d'Artémis
Tempel der Artemis

The Propylaea of the Gymnasium
Les Propylées du Gymnase
Die Propyläen des Gymnasion

40/41
The Temple of Asclepios
◁ Le Temple d'Asclépios
Der Tempel des Asklepios

42
Roman Baths
Bains romains
Römische Bäder

43
The Roman Odeion
L'Odéon romain
Das römische Odeon

45
The Katagogeion (hotel)
Le Katagogeion (hôtel)
Das Katagogeion (Gasthof)

46 NMA
Statue of the Goddess
Hygieia
Statue de la déesse Hygie
Statue der Göttin Hygieia

MUSEUM OF EPIDAUROS
LE MUSEE D'EPIDAURE
DAS MUSEUM VON EPIDAUROS
46—55, 58—67

47

Medical instruments
and various small finds
Instruments médicaux
et divers petits objets
Medizinische Geräte und
verschiedene kleine Funde

ΛΥΧΝΟΙ ΚΑΙ ΑΦΙΕΡΩΜΑΤΑ
LAMPS AND VOTIVE OBJECTS

48

Entablature of Asclepios' Temple restored
Entablement du Temple d'Asclépios restauré
Gesims des Asklepiostempels (restauriert)

50, 51

Acroteria of the temple of Asclepios. Nereids on horseback
▷ ▷ Acrotères du temple d'Asclépios. Des Néréides à cheval
Akroterien des Asklepiostempels. Reitende Nereiden

49 NMA

Asclepios
Asclépios
Asklepios

52 NMA

Penthesile, central figure
of the west pediment of
Asclepios' temple

Penthésilée, figure centrale
du fronton ouest
du temple d'Asclépios

Penthesilea, Zentralfigur
des Westgiebels des
Asklepios-Tempels

53 NMA

Nike, acroterium of
Asclepios' Temple

Nike, acrotère du
Temple d'Asclépios

Nike, Akroterie vom
Asklepiostempel

54

Entablature of Artemis' Temple restored
Entablement restauré du Temple d'Artémis
Gesims des Artemis-Tempels (restauriert)

55
Ornaments of the Tholos
Ornements de la Tholos
Schmuckwerk der Tholos

THE THOLOS OF POLYCLEITOS
LA THOLOS DE POLYCLETE
DIE THOLOS DES POLYKLEITOS
55—67

56/57
▷ ▷ The Tholos or Rotunda
La Tholos ou Rotonde
Die Tholos oder Rotunde

62, 63 THOLOS

Part of the inner corinthian colonnade with its ceiling

Partie de la colonnade corinthienne intérieure avec son plafond à caissons

Teil des inneren korinthischen Säulenganges mit der Kassettendecke

64 T H O L O S

Ornaments of the ceiling of the inner colonnade (detail)

Ornements des caissons du plafond de la colonnade intérieure (détail)

Verzierung der Kassettendecke des inneren Säulenganges (Detail)

65 T H O L O S

Ornaments of the ceiling of the outer colonnade
Ornements des caissons du plafond de la colonnade extérieure
Verzierung der Kassettendecke des äußeren Säulenganges

66 THOLOS

Parts of a corinthian
column and entablature
doric

Parties d'une colonne
Corinthienne et entable-
ment dorique

Teile einer korinthischen
Säule und dorisches
Gesims

67 THOLOS

Corinthian capital
and column

Chapiteau corinthien
et colonne

Korinthisches Kapitell

68

The theatre and the valley of Epidauros
Le théâtre et la vallée d'Epidaure
Das Theater und das Tal von Epidauros

69

The Sanctuary of Asclepios in springtime
Le Sanctuaire d'Asclépios au printemps
Das Heiligtum des Asklepios im Frühling

70
The Theatre
Le Théâtre
Das Theater

THE THE
LE THE
DAS THE
70—79

POLYCLEITOS
POLYCLETE
POLYKLEITOS
70—79

71
The Orchestra
L'orchestre
Die kreisrunde Orchestra

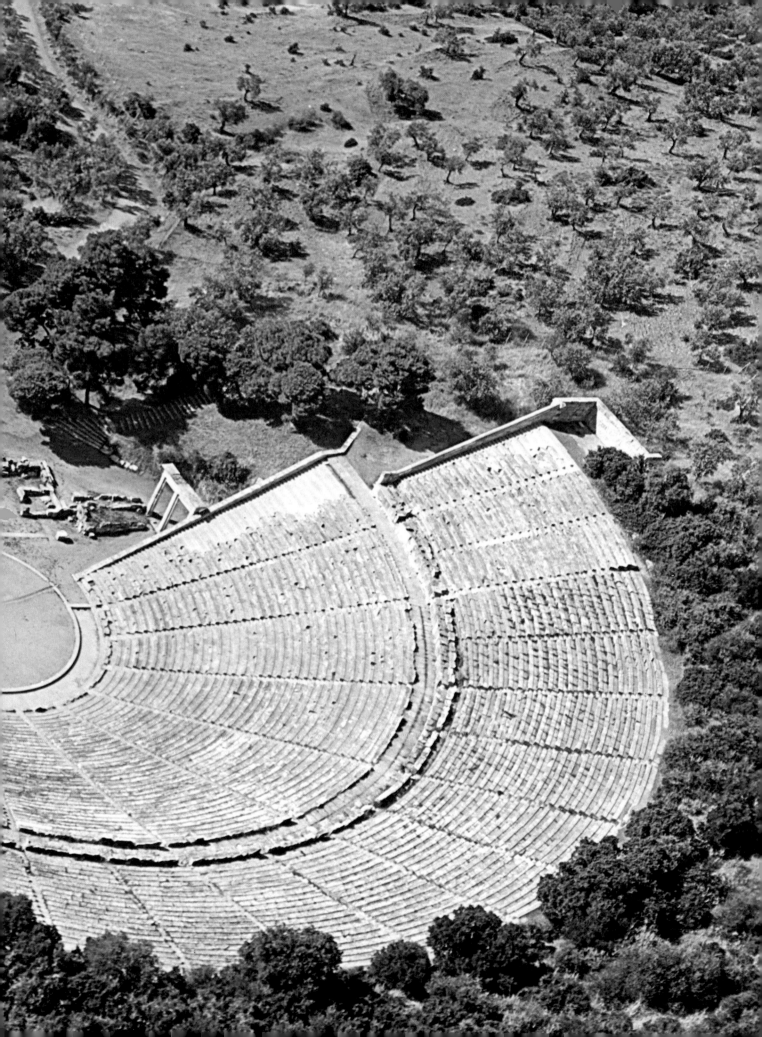

76

Orchestra and proscenium
Orchestre et proscène
Orchestra und Proszenium

77

Part of the theatre's rows
Les gradins du théâtre
Die Sitzreihen des Theater

78/79

Performance of a tragedy in the Theatre
Représentation d'une tragédie au Théâtre   ▷   ▷
Aufführung einer antiken Tragödie im Theater